Saint Mary's Cathedral
LIMERICK

Contents

Foreword from the Bishop — 4
Message from the Dean — 6

- A Brief History of an Ancient Cathedral — 8
- The Treasury — 14
- Monuments — 17
- The Bells — 20
- Misericords — 23
- Music — 27
- The People — 31
- The Graveyard — 33
- Windows — 36

Acknowledgements and Photographic Credits — 40

Foreword from the Bishop

Any Bishop, certainly in the Anglican context, writes a foreword as a guide to 'his' or 'her' cathedral with a certain trepidation. The Dean, after all, is the person really in charge within its walls. The Bishop may make liturgical appearances on certain occasions, and the building has its very name because of the presence of the Bishop's *cathedra*, or teaching chair (see p.13 for image). That said, the Bishop is always, to a certain extent, a visitor, mindful that, when newly arriving in the diocese, it is necessary literally to hammer on the West Door with the crosier and beseech the Dean and the Chapter to be let in.

It is precisely because my role never allows me to lose the eye of the visitor that I welcome this guide so warmly. I always try to approach the glories of Saint Mary's with a fresh eye. Its interior light is never the same on two days of the year, and there is always some new detail to be noticed. Those who (like me) are less challenged by the relentless demands of its maintenance are able to sit back in the balm of its holiness.

I therefore commend this excellent guide, a true labour of love on the part of its compilers, to my fellow visitors. Enjoy this amazing building, let it even allow you to fall to your knees, and go on your way refreshed and rejoicing. And be thankful (again like me) that the Dean, Chapter, Vestry and staff care for it so splendidly, and that they were thrilled today to let *you* in, as yet another welcome pilgrim who came expectantly knocking!

The Right Rev'd Michael A.J. Burrows
Bishop of Limerick

A Message from the Dean

Welcome to Saint Mary's Cathedral. For over eight centuries it has been many things to many people. When the Vikings established the city of Limerick in 922 AD, they established their 'thingmote', or meeting place, on the site now occupied by the Cathedral. It had become the Royal Palace of the Kings of Thomond by 1168, when the last king, Domhnall Mór O'Brien, gifted it to the Church. Over the succeeding centuries the building grew in importance and appearance, leading to the magnificent space that now dominates the Limerick skyline. Set in the heart of medieval Limerick, Saint Mary's has witnessed sieges, famines, wars, conflicts, epidemics and revolutions, as well as growth, development, peace and prosperity.

The Cathedral possesses many fine monuments, windows, treasures and artefacts, each telling its own tale. The graveyard that surrounds the Cathedral is the resting place of kings, princes, mayors, captains of industry, actors, prelates, orphans and entrepreneurs, and in its own way reflects the rich and diverse history of Limerick.

Today, the Cathedral continues to be a house of prayer, with services held here daily. The life of the city is very much part of the worshipping life of the Cathedral as it seeks to be a place of welcome, hospitality, solace and peace to stranger and pilgrim. Reflecting its historic multipurpose use, the Cathedral is a venue for tourism, talks, tours, concerts, exhibitions and recitals. These events emphasise the greater civic role the Cathedral plays within the city, but may also gently point the attendee to something far greater than ourselves – that wonderful presence of the numinous that inspired our forebears and continues to inspire us today.

This booklet was written to deepen the reader's knowledge of this fascinating place and to share with the wider public the wonders over which we are privileged to have custodianship. I thank the editor and contributors who have given lovingly of their time and talents to this project and commend this booklet to a wide and appreciative audience.

The Very Rev'd Niall J.W. Sloane
Dean of Limerick

A Brief History of an Ancient Cathedral

The stones of Saint Mary's Cathedral, Limerick are a record of its long and fascinating history. It is believed to be one of the first churches in Ireland designed and purposely built as a 'great cathedral', and it has continued in this use as a place of worship virtually uninterrupted over the course of more than 850 years. As Thomas Westropp wrote of the Cathedral, in 1898, '[I]ts confused architecture recall[s] nearly every period of the seven centuries that have passed since its foundations were laid.'

Dedicated to the Blessed Virgin Mary, the Cathedral stands proudly on the highest point of King's Island at the heart of the medieval city of Limerick. For over nine centuries, its venerable walls have witnessed the development of Limerick City from its Hiberno-Norse origins through successive invasions by Irish kings and Anglo-Norman invaders, as well as the tumultuous period of the Reformation in the 16th century. It endured also the bloody sieges of Limerick by Cromwell and William of Orange in the 17th century that gave the city its motto, *Urbs Antiqua Fuit Asperrima Belli*, 'an ancient city well-versed in the arts of war'.

Its original foundation can be dated to 1111, during the episcopate of Bishop Gille, when Limerick was ruled by King

King Domhnall Mór O'Brien watches over the Cathedral.

The great West Door.

Murtaugh O'Brien, a descendant of Brian Boru. That year, Gille acted as Legate to Pope Paschal II at the Synod of Ráth Breasail, which divided Ireland into modern dioceses, including the See of Limerick. It was decreed that the church of Saint Mary would become the principal church of the Diocese of Limerick.

The great Romanesque West Door may date from this period, though archaeological excavations show that the sandstone doorway is not in its original location, as earlier burials were uncovered beneath it. Excavations also discovered earlier church foundations at the crossing of the south transept, and the skewed alignment of the south aisle of the modern Cathedral may be a remnant of the foundations of the original Cathedral.

In the mid- to late 12th century Saint Mary's was completely rebuilt and enlarged considerably in the Burgundian style favoured by the Cistercian order, and the traditional foundation date for the Cathedral is given as 1168. The Cathedral was re-constructed in a cruciform plan,

The west end of the Cathedral.

with the chancel and high altar to the east, north and south transepts at the crossing or choir, and the main body of the Church (the nave) to the west, altogether forming the shape of a cross. This building phase was undertaken over many years and was likely begun by Turlough Mac Dermot O'Brien and completed by his son Domhnall Mór O'Brien, the last King of Munster and Limerick, prior to the Norman conquest of the city.

The nave's four arched arcades (leading to the side aisles and the clerestory windows, with the 'Monk's Walk' above the arches) date to this period. The square piers with scalloped decoration are indicative of mid-12th-century design. The earlier Romanesque West Door was incorporated into the new building, with a spiral staircase to the south leading to the clerestory walk above the nave, and there was no tower above the west end of the Cathedral at this phase of construction.

The decorated coffin lid from the grave of Domhnall Mór O'Brien, who died in 1194, can be seen in the chancel, on the north side of the Lady Chapel.

Following the Anglo-Norman conquest of the city in 1195, the next development to the Cathedral was made in the early 13th century, with the construction of a sacristy to the north of the chancel, where the Blue Coat School now stands. As well as this, the nave's westernmost pillars were strengthened to support an enlarged western front, possibly containing a belfry.

One of the great early benefactors to the Cathedral was John Budstone, who in 1360 had a new chapel, dedicated to Saint Mary Magdelene, constructed to the east of the south transept, where the chapter house now stands. The Budstone sedilia, a beautiful triple-arched recess with trefoil heads commemorating his family, is located in the south transept. A chapel dedicated to Saint James was built adjacent to the Saint Mary Magdelene Chapel c.1369.

In the late 14th century, additions were made to the north side of the Cathedral, with the construction of two small chapels dedicated to SS Catherine and Nicholas located to the west of the north transept. These chapels were later much enlarged to create the 'Arthur' or 'Jebb' Chapel that survives to this day.

In the early 15th century, a pair of twin lancet windows with cinquefoil detail above were inserted into the north and south walls of the chancel, giving more light to the high altar in the Lady Chapel. To strengthen the walls of the chancel due to the insertion of these windows, a set of four buttresses were built against the east end of the Cathedral.

In the 16th century, the south aisles of the Cathedral were extended to create three separate chapels, one dedicated to Saint Anne, and the others named after wealthy merchant families: Stritch and Sexten. The pitched gables of these chapels obscured many of the clerestory windows on the Cathedral's south side. These chapels were later combined to create a large and open Consistorial or Bishop's Court. This area is now used for exhibitions and installations throughout the year.

THE REFORMATION

In the first half of the 16th century, King Henry VIII placed himself as Head of the Church in England, thus establishing Anglicanism. This movement spread to Ireland, which was mainly under English rule by this time. In due course Henry suppressed the monasteries and took over their properties, accumulating their wealth.

Saint Mary's Cathedral was one such property. In 1538, Lord Grey was sent to Limerick to ensure that Henry VIII's decrees were endorsed. Following the Cromwellian invasion in 1651, the army stabled their horses in the Cathedral, doing damage to the Cathedral fabric that can still be seen.

A plaque detailing the Reformation-era damage.

Saint George's Chapel.

Also known as the O'Brien Chapel, it is reputedly the burial place of the notorious Lord Inchiquin, also known as Murrough of the Burnings, and Richard Talbot, the Earl of Tyrconnell, who died during the second Williamite siege in 1691.

The next phase of the Cathedral's development, in the mid-16th century, saw the construction of chapels to the north and south sides of the west end of the building. These structures gave the Cathedral the rectangular plan that survives to this day, concealing the cruciform shape of its plan that had originated in the 12th century. The building to the north was a chapel dedicated to the Creagh family. This later became the Baptistery and is now the location of the Cathedral's gift shop.

Completing the Cathedral's rectangular plan on the south side is Saint George's Chapel. The ceiling of this building retains its stunning painted decoration, and a spiral staircase to the west leads to a Solar, or bishop's residential room. Saint George's Chapel is also known as the Glentworth or Pery chapel, as it holds the vault of the Earls of Limerick. Above the entrance to the chapel hangs a set of chain-shot (cannon balls) dating to the Williamite sieges of 1690/1 and believed to have been found embedded in the Cathedral's walls.

On the north side of the Cathedral, to the west of Saint Catherine's Chapel, a building was constructed in the form of a fortified castle-like tower house more commonly seen in the countryside. At two or three storeys high, a machicolation (defensive structure) can be seen on the western side of the Arthur Chapel, built outside the Cathedral building to defend the corner of the tower house. The tower house was later lowered and converted into Saint Mark's Chapel. On the west wall of the chapel you can see a mullioned window, splayed inwards, which once would have looked over the River Shannon but now looks into the Baptistery.

The intricately constructed vaulted ceiling of Saint Mark's Chapel is one of the Cathedral's most beautiful features.

Pictorial evidence, dating to the 17th century, shows a two-storey porch building attached to the south side of the Cathedral. This porch became the main entrance to the Cathedral, accessed from the High Street by a laneway called Bachelor's Walk and from Bridge Street by Cross Lane, named after the Knights

A set of chain-shot dating to the Williamite sieges of 1690/1.

Templar of the White Cross, who had a frank-house or hostel next to the Cathedral in the late 13th century.

Compared to other cathedrals, many of which underwent substantial rebuilding projects in line with Victorian principles of 'restoration', Saint Mary's experienced a rather light-touch and ad hoc approach throughout the 19th century. Various architects were involved in drawing up plans for the Cathedral during this century, including renowned Gothic architect George Edmond Street, but none of these plans were ever fully realised.

At the beginning of the century, a new porch was erected over the West Door, but it was criticised almost immediately and was finally removed in 1898. By the middle of the century, at least three of the recessed arches were heavily restored in line with Victorian practices at the time. The eastern elevation also underwent numerous alterations during this century. Around 1859, work had begun on the current reredos and windows, a triple lancet arrangement with twin trilobes.

Saint Mary's appears to be unique to Ireland as a medieval cathedral that survived the 19th century without any major reconstruction work carried out on the fabric. The Cathedral remains an eclectic, varied building whose fascinating and long history can be read from the stones that have remained in place.

An interior view of the Cathedral, c.1860, with the domed *cathedra* on the left.

The Treasury

The treasury has the most important collection of 17th- and 18th-century locally made Limerick silver. The importance is highlighted in that many of the silversmiths and donor families were baptised, married and buried either in Saint Mary's, Saint Munchin's or Saint John's Churches. Saint Mary's was also the place of worship for many of these silversmiths and donors. The treasury is a great source of information to researchers in identifying the makers and their marks, and has silver by prominent 17th-century Dublin silversmiths and an example of a 17th-century unrecorded London silversmith. There are a number of pieces of church plate that belonged to other churches in the diocese and which are now deconsecrated. There are also examples of 17th-century church plate by two eminent Limerick silversmiths: John Bucknor, the first Limerick silversmith to use a punch for his maker's mark, 'I.B.' flanged by three stars and a punch for the 'Town Mark' (a castle) gateway between two towers in the 1660s; and James Robinson, whose maker's mark was 'I.R.' in script conjoined, an eight-pointed star and a castle, all in irregular punches.

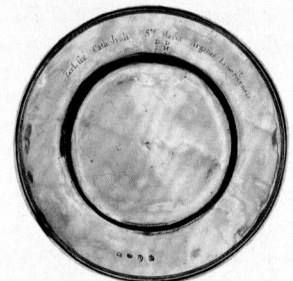
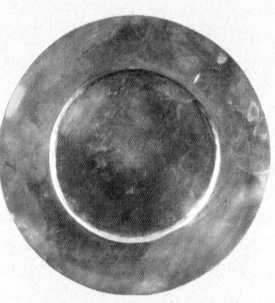

- **The Seal of the Dean and Chapter (2017)**
  This piece was made by Gleeson Goldsmiths in Shannon, Co. Clare for Dean Sloane and is worn by the Dean of Limerick.

- **The Saint Mary's Bread Plate (1676)**
  Silver circular plain dish-shaped bread plate with reeded border. Diameter: 25.4cm. Weight: 15oz.

  Mark: Maker's mark 'P.P.' in a shield; Leopard's head crowned; Lion passant; Date letter 'P' for 1672–3.

  An unrecorded London silversmith.

  Inscription: '*Ecclesiae Cathdrali Stae Mariae Virginis Limericensis*', '*D-D. I-H. 1676*' (the initials possibly refer to the donor(s)).

- **Paten by John Bucknor (c.1665)**
  Plain circular dis-shaped paten with a wide rim. No inscription.

◆ **The Smith Flagon (1711)**
A large silver flagon with tapered cylindrical body on a moulded foot with an applied rim on top and an applied reeded band above the foot. The hollow tapering 'S' scroll handle is decorated on top with an applied 'rat-tail' and a raised thumbpiece below the hinge in the form of a double corkscrew.

Maker: James Robinson, Limerick 'J.R.' monogram in a shield (1679–1715).

Inscription: '*The Gift of Mrs. Dorathea Smith to the Church of St. Munchins May 1st 1711*'.

Dorathea Smith was the wife of Thomas Smith, Bishop of Limerick (1695–1715). This flagon was donated three months before she died on 6 August 1711. She is buried in Saint Munchin's Church, where there is a monument erected to her memory over the Smith family vault.

◆ **Marsh Communion Cup (1671)**
Silver communion cup with a deep beaker-shaped tapered bowl on a spreading trumpet foot which is soldered to the bowl. It has decoration of pointillé work around both the bowl and the foot. Inscription: '*Sacris Sti Munchini Limeric D Dq Humillima Jesu Serva Maria Marsh 1671*'.

Maria Marsh was the daughter of Jeremy Taylor, Bishop of Down, Conor and Dromore (1661–7). She married Francis Marsh, Bishop of Limerick (1667–73) and Archbishop of Dublin (1682–93). He died in 1693 and is buried in Christ Church Cathedral, Dublin.

◆ **The Williamson Flagon (*c.*1700)**
This silver flagon has a hollow 'S' scroll handle, raised shell thumbpiece, domed lid and trumpet-shaped spreading foot.

Maker's mark: 'I.R.' conjoined script for James Robinson, Limerick silversmith.

Engraved with the Arms of Williamson impaling Lennox surmounted by a scroll bearing the motto 'SUB UMBRA ALA RVM TUARUM'.

Inscription: '*Ex Dono Josephi Williamson Equitis Aurati Ecclesiae Cathedrali Beatae Mariae Virginis Limericencis*'.

Sir Joseph Williamson sat in the Irish House of Parliament (1692–5) and as an MP for Co. Clare and for Limerick until 1699. He married Catherine Stuart (Baroness Clifton), widow of Henry O'Brien, Lord Ibrackan. Williamson died in 1701 and was buried in Westminster Abbey, where he was joined by his wife a year later.

◆ **Plate (1795)**
Silver bread plate inscribed 'St Mary's Limerick 1795'.

The Treasury

◆ **The Cornelius O'Dea Mitre and Crosier**
Cornelius O'Dea was consecrated Bishop of Limerick in 1400 and resigned in 1426. He died in 1434 and was buried in Saint Mary's Cathedral. The jewelled mitre and crosier, mostly made of silver, were made to the order of Cornelius O'Dea in 1418. Only the mitre bears the engraved signature of the maker: 'Thomas O'Carryd, artifex facients.' Thomas O'Carryd may be Thomas O'Carty, who is mentioned by Gilbert in 'The Callender of Ancient Records of Dublin' as a goldsmith in that city in 1418. They are regarded as the greatest medieval treasures of Limerick, and their survival during the sieges and turmoil of the city is extraordinary. The O'Dea Mitre and Crosier are on display nearby in the Hunt Museum, Rutland Street, Limerick.

Monuments

Many of the Cathedral's monuments are in memory of loved ones sadly lost in wars all over the world. Others commemorate the good deeds of benefactors who have passed through this ancient place over the centuries.

In all, there are over 80 monuments on the walls and floors of the Cathedral, including ones memorialising the O'Briens, founders of this great building, and the Barringtons, who founded Barrington's Hospital and built Glenstal Castle (now Glenstal Abbey). The earliest memorial to the Barrington family is located in the graveyard and dedicated to Francis Barrington, who died in 1683. It is generally accepted that he was the father of Samuel Barrington, the clock and chime maker. There is also a monument in memory of Samuel Barrington: a small, discreet stone on the south-west pillar dated 1693.

There are nine memorials to the Maunsell family. Robert and his brother Thomas Maunsell were the founders of the Maunsell Bank in 1789. Robert's bust is on a pedestal on the south-east pillar of the nave in the Cathedral. Another member of the family founded an Anglican nunnery, while others are commemorated for their involvement with the military.

The fine statue of Bishop Jebb was executed by the eminent sculptor Edward Hodges Bailey. Another sculpture of interest is the Westropp Reredos on the east wall of the south transept (Saint James' Chapel), which had been exhibited at the 1862 International Exhibition. It consists of a triple arcade, where the centre panel is a representation of the Resurrection, and on

The Westropp Reredos.

Memorial to Bishop John Jebb.

The Cleeve Angel.

either side, the Agony in the Garden and the Entombment. The work was carried out by James Redfern of London.

The Galwey, Stritch, Bultingfort Memorial (located in Saint James' Chapel) is a tomb erected by Edmund, son of Geofrey Galwey and Margaret, daughter of Richard Bultingfort. Richard Bultingfort was Mayor of Limerick in 1376, 1380 and 1386. There are four shields of families, allied by intermarriage, connected with this monument.

The Cleeve Angel, likely the most photographed piece in the Cathedral, was brought inside from the head of the Cleeve grave because of deterioration. It is now at the Cathedral's west end. The Cleeve family provided work for thousands of Limerick people in their factories, which produced milk, cheese, canned food and toffee. The business closed in 1923.

Saint George's Chapel, at the west end of the Cathedral, is the burial place of the Earls of Limerick. There are many monuments to this family, but the beautiful sculpture of Lord Edmond Henry Glentworth, the work of Richard Westmacott of London, is a very special piece.

Two war memorials on the south-west wall commemorate those who died in the First and Second World War. There is a simple memorial to William Dermod O'Brien PRHA and his brother Conor, architect, voyager, author – descendants of the founder of the Cathedral. Conor designed the screen to the Lady Chapel in memory of Viscount Glentworth and his sister, Lady Victoria Brady.

An imposing monument in the chancel area (to the North of the High Altar) has the mutilated remains of the effigy of Earl of Thomond Lord Donagh O'Brien, and that of his Countess, Lady Elizabeth Fitzgerald. The monument as it stands retains little of the original structure, having been defaced during a time of unrest.

There are two well-executed monuments to members of the Lloyd family: a large white marble monument in the Chapel of Saint Catherine in memory of Lieutenant Colonel Richard Lloyd, who died in the south of France in 1813; and one on a pillar in the Consistorial Court, in memory of Captain Eyre Lloyd 2nd Coldstream Guards, who lost his life in a voluntary attempt to reach his wounded officer in Transvaal, 1901.

There is a rather unusual memorial to the poet Daniel Hayes on the south side, south aisle pillar. It is said that Hayes left instructions for the monument's wording but left room for his friends to add their own kind words to the large, long monument, but, sadly, no one ever did. After obtaining his degree from Trinity College, Dublin, Hayes studied for the Bar and entered Middle Temple, London, where he led a fashionable life. Upon his death in 1767, he bequeathed the greater part of his property to the County of Limerick Hospital (now the School of Music), but owing to certain informalities, his intentions were frustrated. This hospital at that time was located outside the walls in Saint Francis Abbey, founded by Giles Vandeleur and Sylvester O'Halloran on land given by Sexton Pery at a peppercorn rent. It moved to Mulgrave Street in 1811. Hayes's remains are interred in the Cathedral.

On the south-west wall is a memorial to George Fredrick Handel Rogers, who was an organist in the Cathedral for 50 years. Rogers gathered round him a group of zealous, accomplished choristers. He had a music school on Henry Street and his family members were all accomplished musicians. Rogers died 1892 and is buried in Saint Munchin's Churchyard.

Memorial to the Earl of Thomond.

Memorial to George F.H. Rogers.

On a pillar in the north-west is a black marble monument in memory of William Yorke, a prominent citizen of Limerick during the mid-17th century. He was three times Mayor of Limerick and was noted for philanthropic and charitable work amongst the poor. His name is chiefly associated with the Cathedral in connection with the bells, having in the year 1673 presented a peal of six, on which the tenor has his name engraved.

The Bells

The Cathedral Tower is home to the famous bells of Saint Mary's, which have witnessed all the changes of Limerick's chaotic history, pealing forth in joy and in sorrow, for festival and funeral, bringing pleasure or consolation to all with their mellow tones.

The Cathedral bells hold a special place in the hearts of all Limerick people, as their distinctive sound can be heard every Sunday morning, calling parishioners to worship. But the bells are also rung for many civic and cultural events. One of the old customs is for the bells of Saint Mary's to ring in the New Year. Late on New Year's Eve the ringers ascend the tower, while citizens of the city gather in the streets below to await the tenor bell tolling the 12 strokes of midnight, before being joined by the remaining bells.

The bells are rung by a dedicated group of ringers, who have won many awards at bell-ringing competitions over the years. The ringers are rightly proud not only of their skills but of their ecumenical traditions, as they and the ringers of Mount Saint Alphonsus have assisted each other in ringing bells, long before ecumenism was developed.

The tower, located at the Cathedral's western end, dates from the 15th century, as does the belfry, which contains the famous eight bells. The first reference to the Cathedral bells dates from the time

The bells.

of John Budstone (or Buston), who was Bailiff of Limerick. He was a wealthy and prominent citizen and a liberal benefactor of Saint Mary's, and it is recorded that he presented four brass bells to the Cathedral in 1401.

The next reference to the bells in the Cathedral records is in 1673, when William Yorke presented six bells to Saint Mary's. Yorke, who was of Dutch origin, was an alderman and three times Mayor of Limerick. Yorke's bells were cast, most likely in the grounds of the Cathedral, by the noted bell-founders William and Roger Perdue, who came from Gloucestershire.

It is probable that Budstone's bells were used in the casting of Yorke's peal. William Perdue died while engaged in this work and was buried in Saint Mary's Cathedral. The initials of William and Roger Perdue were inscribed on the third bell (until 1923, when it was recast) with these words in Latin: *Vivat Rex et Floreat Grex Anno Domini 1673 W.P. R.P.*

In 1703, two more bells were added to Yorke's peal by Tobias and Edward Covey, who are reputed to have been descendants of the Perdues. This addition most likely involved the provision of a new oak frame to house the bells. This frame holds the current bells. It is on record that the eight bells rang out in 1712 to welcome James, Duke of Ormonde, and Lord Lieutenant of Ireland, to Limerick.

Extensive renovations were carried out on the belfry in 1937/8. The oak beams that supported the bell frames, having deteriorated, were replaced by two massive steel girders that are deeply embedded in the tower walls. The first, second and seventh bells were recast with generous financial aid from Everard Hewson, and new bearings and gudgeons were fitted to all the bells. A modern chiming apparatus was also installed, and this can be rung by one person when a team of ringers is not available.

The fifth and sixth bells, which were cast by T. Meares of London in 1829, are now the oldest bells in the tower. Saint Mary's today has a peal of eight bells in the key of F sharp, with the tenor (heaviest) weighing in at 24 cwt (over 1,200 kg).

Above:
The call bell.

Misericords

In the Middle Ages, as today, one of the principal functions of the Cathedral was the continuing offering of the liturgy, in its content and in its context a daily illustration of the beauty of holiness.

In times past there would have been a larger collegiate-style residential community around the Cathedral to participate in the daily liturgical round, the *Opus Dei*. There would have been the dignitaries, other members of the chapter, sometimes the Bishop, lesser clergy, whose duty was mainly to act as singers.

At the heart of the Daily Office, offered several times a day in neo-monastic style, was the hearing and indeed the singing of Scripture. This involved a large amount of psalmody on each occasion, sung mainly in plainsong and derivative styles, and it all took quite a long time! After the Reformation, the use of the Psalter was reshaped, so that in cathedrals it was sung in its entirety once a month. Thus, on the fifteenth evening of each month, Psalm 78 was used – all 73 verses of it.

In all of this, there emerged an interesting conflation of devotion and common sense, of practical need and the opportunity for artistic imagination. Clergy were meant to stand for the psalms and for many other prayers, and this could be arduous, especially for older priests. But it was important that, from the vantage point of the congregation, they did not appear to give in to the need to sit down.

So it was in many places the custom that the stalls/seats on which the chapter members sat, were hinged, and the seat was raised during long periods of devotion. On the underside of the seat

An eagle.

An angel.

was provided a carved lip, on which aged canons could rest their posteriors. Thus, although the congregation perceived them to be standing, the priests were in fact being comfortably supported as the phrases of psalmody and prayer washed over them. These carved lips came to be known as 'misericords', a rather humorous recognition of the misery and discomfort from which they delivered their occupants.

This added feature led to a distinctive addition where decoration is concerned. Although there are many examples of this decoration in cathedrals across Europe, in Ireland there is nothing surviving to rival what we see in Limerick. Medieval wood carvers, whose imagination tended to run riot but who sometimes preferred to leave their most curious and at times even grotesque endeavours in places where they would not be overly prominent (gargoyles to remove rain from the roof being another example), began to decorate the misericords elaborately, no doubt to the delight and amusement of those who endured long bouts of psalmody while perched on them.

They decorated the misericords with human heads, animals both real and imaginary, elaborate foliage and, at times, of course, with rich Christian symbolism. The misericords in Saint Mary's, carved in oak from Cratloe, Co. Clare (wood from the same forest was also used in the roof beams of Westminster Hall, London and the Royal Palace, Amsterdam) and probably dating from *c.*1480 to 1500, are an elaborate celebration of the variety and profligacy of God's creation, carried out with ingenuity and even playfulness. What follows is a brief tour, providing a few examples from this unique and varied collection.

Misericords

◆ On the west wall of the north transept, the carving nearest the corner depicts a griffin, a creature believed to be of amazing size and strength, capable of carrying a live ox in its talons, with the fore part of an eagle and the hind quarters of a lion.

◆ Two stalls to your left, you encounter a splendidly carved swan, a frequent symbol of martyrdom in the Middle Ages, as it was widely believed that swans only sang when taking their dying breaths.

◆ Move one more stall to your left, and you find two antelopes with intricately intertwined necks.

◆ Cross to the east wall of the transept, and three stalls in from the corner you find a lion in conflict with a wyvern, a mythical dragon-like monster. This beast, symbolising evil and destruction, is being overcome by the lion, itself reminding us of the triumphant Lion of Judah, Christ himself.

Misericords

- To your right is the head of a young man with a distinctive headdress fashionable in the 15th century, the chaperon, with the hair piled up on top of the head and covered with a twisted hood.

- Moving one further stall to your right you see another fictional monster, the Manticora, thought to have the face of a human, the body of a lion, the wings of an eagle and the tail of a scorpion. It supposedly devoured human flesh.

- The final carving to your right at the end of the row of stalls is another human head, supposedly a representation of King Henry IV, who had reigned earlier in the 15th century.

A Cockatrice.

There are many more, so go feast your eyes and let your imagination run riot as you explore these timber jewels from the heritage of Limerick.

Music

Sacred choral music has been sung in Saint Mary's Cathedral for the past eight centuries, a tradition that continues to the present day. The current cathedral choir is made up of a number of secondary school and third level students (choral scholars), who are supported by professional singers (vicars choral) and some volunteers. In recent years it has been possible to establish fruitful links with the Limerick School of Music, the Irish World Academy of Music and Dance (IWAMD, at the University of Limerick) and Mary Immaculate College.

Several choral scholars have been students on the unique UL Master's course in Ritual Chant and Song at IWAMD, and this creates a direct link back to the medieval music that would have been sung in services since the earliest years of the Cathedral's history.

The first indications of liturgical practice in Saint Mary's occur in the constitutions establishing the chapter of canons enacted

The choir sings during a clergy Procession.

Choral music has been an integral part of the Cathedral since its foundation.

by Bishop Donatus Ua Briain *c.*1205. A college of 10 minor canons or vicars choral was founded during the tenure of Bishop Hubert de Burgh, 1222–*c.*1250, and confirmed by decree of the chapter in 1272. This college lasted well into the 19th century, and has recently been re-established (February 2024). Prior to this, there had been no vicar choral appointed since 1946. The presence from the 13th century of a body of vicars choral suggests significant proficiency in both sacred music and liturgical practice.

Bishop Hubert also allocated financial resources towards the purchase and repair of books and vestments for the Cathedral. This is of liturgical importance because it demonstrates that, in common with other Irish cathedrals, the liturgy was influenced from an early date by that of the church of Salisbury, otherwise known as the Use of Sarum. This variant of the Roman rite was in use in Ireland from the 12th century onwards.

The Sarum liturgy was renowned for its elaborate ceremonies and in particular its use of Processions, something for which the space at Saint Mary's is well suited. Present-day congregations experience this at the annual Procession on the evening of Advent Sunday.

The earliest reference to payment of an organist in the Cathedral occurs during the episcopate of Bishop John Mothel, 1459–72. It is recorded that an organ was gifted by Bishop Bernard Adams, Bishop from 1604 to 1626.

The fortunes of the cathedral choir at Saint Mary's have risen and fallen through the centuries. One high point was in the period after the Restoration of the English monarchy in 1660, during the reign of Charles II, 1660–85, when a grant was made to the Dean and Chapter of Saint Mary's for 'the constant support and maintenance of a sufficient and able choir to serve in the Cathedral'. This enabled the provision of a sizeable musical establishment: in addition to six vicars choral (five of whom were in holy orders), there were five salaried choirmen and six choristers. While the chapter did not make any direct monetary payment to the boys, they did provide clothing and schooling.

The boys' tuition was provided at a Blue Coat [charity] School, which was built onto the north-east side of the Cathedral. This fine room is still in daily use as the rehearsal and music room for the current cathedral choir. The choristers were subsequently apprenticed out to the trades and received an apprenticeship fee from the Cathedral when they had completed their time in the choir.

It would appear that by the closing years of the 18th century the choral foundation at Saint Mary's was not in such good health. A visitor to the Cathedral, writing in 1797, makes a reference to the choristers as being '8 or 10 poor boys of some charter school dressed as a choir intolerably bad'.

Various improvements were made by successive Deans during the first half of the 19th century, so that by the deanship of Anthony La Touche Kirwan, 1849–68, it was possible to revive daily choral services (in 1852), and by Disestablishment (1 January 1871) there was a stable team of six vicars choral.

Just nine gentlemen served as organist at Saint Mary's during the 256-year period

The choir stalls looking towards the West Door.

The organ looking east.

The organist and choir.

from 1748 to 2004, including several generations of the Osborne family. Between them, four members of this family were organists at Saint Mary's from 1748 to c.1837. George William Osborne (organist 1799–c.1833) was father to the most celebrated member of the family, George Alexander, who was to become renowned not only as an organist but also as a pianist and composer, and counted Berlioz and Chopin amongst his friends.

Subsequent organists included a former assistant organist of Westminster Abbey, Frank Muspratt, and Michael Franklin, who later moved on to be organist of Saint Columb's Cathedral, Derry. Indeed, two organists covered nearly a whole century between them: George Frederick Handel Rogers (for whom there is a memorial plaque in the Cathedral, see p.19) was at Saint Mary's from c.1838 to 1885, and he was succeeded by Mr Muspratt.

In the years following Disestablishment of the Church of Ireland the choir benefited from a bequest made by Bishop Charles Graves. It is recorded 'that in accordance with the traditional usage of many years full public choral services have been and now are duly and reverently conducted (after the use of the Church of Ireland)'.

Those currently entrusted with responsibility for the music and liturgy seek to continue in this spirit. In addition to singing at the weekly services, the cathedral choir also takes part in concerts and performances away from Saint Mary's. There is a regular series of lunchtime concerts at the Cathedral, and together with other concerts and events, the musical ministry of Saint Mary's reaches far out into the ancient city and county of Limerick.

The People

People are at the heart of all the Cathedral's activities – worshippers, benefactors, tourists, volunteers, clergy. Each in their own unique way have and continue to make an impression on Saint Mary's. Over the centuries many people, both international and local, are connected to Saint Mary's Cathedral, some incidentally and others through longevity, within the wider Limerick and Irish context. Here we give a small glimpse into the lives of some of those who have made their mark in this wonderful place.

- The Very Reverend Sandra Pragnell was the first female to hold the post as the 62nd Dean of Saint Mary's Cathedral from 2012 to 2017. From Southampton, England, she moved to Ireland in 1994. Before coming to Limerick, she was rector of a parish in Dundalk, Co. Louth.

- Lady Victoria Brady (née Pery) was born in 1893, to William Pery, 4th Earl of Limerick, and May Pery, Countess of Limerick. Victoria was a pioneering aviator, performing five 'loop the loop' flights at Hendon aerodrome alongside Gustav Hamel, a British aviator. She married James Brady, an American, with whom she had two children. She died in 1918 of influenza.

- Catherine O'Brien was born in 1881 in Co. Clare. Having trained at the Dublin Metropolitan School of Art, she designed two windows in Saint Catherine's Chapel. She was part of the Irish An Túr Gloine (Tower of Glass) movement, a stained glass co-operative. Other of her works are to be seen in churches around Ireland.

The high altar and reredos.

- Frances Condell was the first female Mayor of Limerick, 1962–4. She worked diligently to ensure US President John F. Kennedy's visit to Limerick in 1963. He commented on her witty speech, and indeed she spoke eloquently on his death later that year. She retired from city council life after her second term, devoting her time to causes close to her heart in the city. Condell Road, on the west side of the River Shannon, is named after her. She died in 1986 and is buried in the Cathedral's graveyard.

- Florence Nightingale contributed financially to the stained-glass window created in memory of Augustus Stafford O'Brien, Member of Parliament.

- Robert von Ranke Graves (1895–1985), known as one of the war poets, has connections to Saint Mary's through both his father and grandfather. His father, Alfred Percival Graves, was prominent in the Gaelic Revival. His grandfather, Charles Graves, Bishop of Limerick 1866–99, is interred in the Cathedral grounds.

- Willie Pearse, a mason and sculptor, created the reredos behind the high altar. In it, Jesus Christ is depicted as the Prophet, Priest and Shepherd of His flock. Willie was the brother of Patrick Pearse, teacher and leader of the Easter Rising 1916, for which he was executed.

- Micheál Ó Súilleabháin (1950–2018), noted composer and pianist, founded the Irish World Academy of Music & Dance at the University of Limerick in 1994. He performed in the Cathedral on many occasions.

- Catherine Hayes (1818–1861) was born in Limerick and baptised in Saint Mary's. The Bishop of Limerick at the time, Edmund Knox, noted her singing talent and arranged for her tuition in Dublin. She did further training in Milan, making her debut in Marseille, France. She was the first Irish woman to sing in the Royal Opera Covent Garden, London and at La Scala, Milan. She toured extensively in the Americas and the Pacific region.

Frances Condell with President Kennedy in 1963.

The Graveyard

West wall of the former Limerick City Exchange.

The history of a place is perhaps most evident in the memorials and tributes to those who passed through it. This is certainly the case when one examines the centuries-old graveyard that surrounds Saint Mary's. The graveyard can be divided into three historic periods: the upper sections within the graveyard walls, and within the immediate vicinity of the Cathedral (c.1600–c.1910); the lower section parallel to Bridge Street (c.1880–c.1940); and the two lower sections parallel to Merchant's Quay (from c.1900). The surviving burial registers at Saint Mary's date from c.1700. Since then, over 13,000 burials have been recorded here.

Before the expansion of the grounds surrounding Saint Mary's, burials would have primarily taken place in burial vaults and graves inside the Cathedral itself. Being buried inside the Cathedral was an honour bestowed only on certain individuals – wealthy parishioners and patrons, members of the clergy, and Bishops. Examples of these burial monuments can be seen inside the Cathedral, and around the Shaw Memorial, to the left before the West Door entrance.

Walking around the graveyard, one walks through some of the original streets and lanes of medieval Limerick. Names like Grid Iron Lane and Bachelor's Walk now form part of the paths and walkways around the grounds of the Cathedral. Before the expansion of the graveyard in the 19th century, many buildings stood on the land surrounding the Cathedral. Today, there is little trace of these structures, apart from two points of interest.

The present surviving remains of the façade of the Limerick City Exchange (a covered market place and home to

The Ireton stone pinnacles.

Detail from the Sexton tomb.

the council chamber), which forms the eastern boundary of the graveyard, was built in 1777 on the grounds of the Cathedral to widen the street to facilitate horse-drawn carriages. This replaced the exchange, which was rebuilt in 1702 after being damaged during the Williamite siege. Another, perhaps more subtle reminder of the history of the graveyard are two plainly decorated stone pinnacles, situated at the end of the south walkway. These were originally atop the gable of a house at the south-eastern corner of the graveyard. This house was reputedly the place where Henry Ireton, son-in-law of Oliver Cromwell, succumbed to the plague in November 1651, during a siege of the city as part of the Cromwellian conquest of Ireland.

Walking through the graveyard means retracing centuries of Limerick's history. Many graves, both prominent and discreet, tell the story of Limerick and its people, as well as the way in which the city evolved socially and economically. Prominent limestone tombs, such as those of the Boyd, Sexton, Barrington and Myles families, dominate the landscape of the graveyard, the idea behind using tombs over graves.

The magnificent Celtic Cross is in memory of Bishop Graves, one-time Bishop of Limerick. His epitaph is written in three languages – in Latin by R.G. Tyrell (Vice-Provost of Dublin University), in Irish by Douglas Hyde (President of Ireland 1938–45) and in English by his son, A.P. Graves, who wrote the song 'Father O'Flynn'. On the cross are symbols of the Pascal Lamb and the Four Evangelists, along with the epitaph.

Also buried here are the parents and some of the children of John Ferrar, who wrote and published *An History of the City of Limerick* in 1767 and founded the *Limerick Chronicle* in 1768, as well as members of the Creagh family, who were among the earliest recorded great merchants of Limerick. They provided Mayors of Limerick on 32 occasions and Bailiffs/Sheriffs on 58 occasions, as well as two Bishops. There are also many Arthurs: merchants who held municipal offices in the city and became great benefactors to the Cathedral, where they also served on a number of occasions as Bishops and authored *The Arthur Manuscript*. A memorial with their armorial can be found in the graveyard, where there is a memorial to Thomas Arthur as well.

Other noteworthy graves, to mention just a few, include those of Frances Condell, the first female Mayor of Limerick; Prince Milo Petrović-Njegoš, a member of the Montenegrin royal family; and Dr Samuel Crumpe, one of the first physicians

The Celtic Cross in memory of Bishop Graves.

to investigate the effects of opium as a stimulant on the human body. One must also remember that, given the age of the graveyard, many of its burials are unmarked. From examining the burial registers here, it is evident that people from all classes of society were buried here, many of whom did not have a headstone or memorial erected. The United Nations Memorial Garden to the west of the Cathedral is also worth noting.

Windows

Originally, stained-glass windows in a church or a cathedral were for teaching and reminding the people of Bible stories. Over the centuries this continued, with the added sponsorship of prominent families who worshipped in the churches. Saint Mary's Cathedral has many fine windows which were financed by important families in Limerick City and the surrounding area.

- **Westropp Window (or Old Testament Window)** (south transept)
  The five lights, or panels, in this spectacular window show some of the doings of Noah, Abraham, Moses, David and Solomon. This one is of interest to children in particular, as it includes some of the animals from Noah's Ark.

- **Edwards Window** (beside Saint George's Chapel)
  This window depicts the Crucifixion (*He was delivered for our offences*) and the Resurrection (*And was raised for our Justification*) in memory of Isabella Edwards, wife of Rev. Arthur Edwards, Vicar Choral of Saint Mary's. This in itself is unusual in a Church of Ireland cathedral, as it depicts the crucified Jesus Christ.

- **Glentworth Windows** (Saint George's Chapel)
  These two windows depict scriptural scenes, including the Crucifixion and the Resurrection. The three-light window shows the Agony in the Garden, the Transfiguration, the Scourging and Christ Bearing the Cross. The window is presumed to be in memory of one of the Earls of Limerick or some member of the Pery family. The two-light window is in memory of Edmund, Viscount Glentworth (*I heard a voice from heaven saying: Blessed are the dead who die in the Lord*).

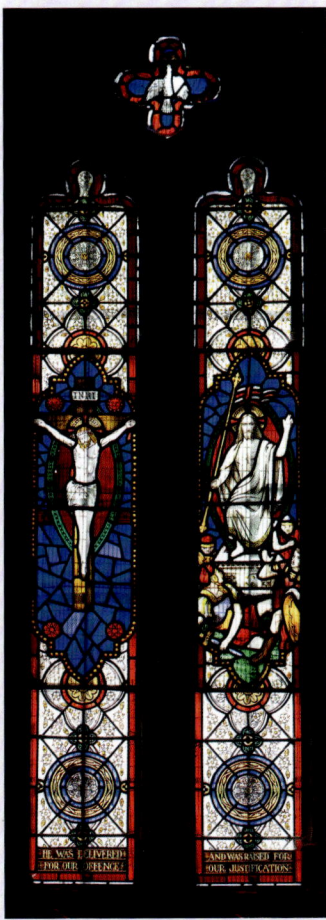

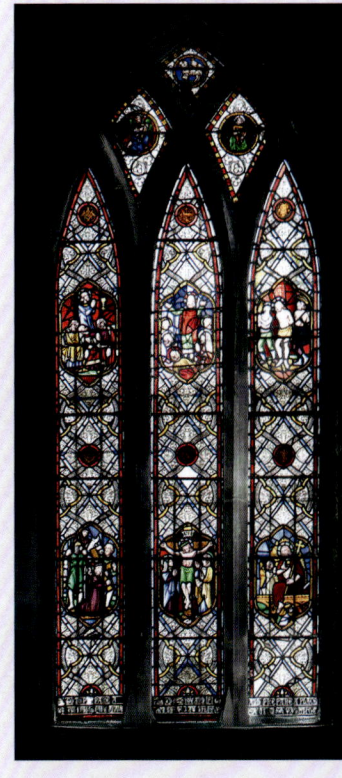

Windows

- **McKern Window** (south chapel)
Saint Mary's has a long tradition of musical excellence. This window is a memorial to John McKern, a chorister with a fine bass voice of unusual beauty and quality. It is fitting that it shows Jubal playing the pan pipes and David the harp. The angels at the top hold a scroll reading *Sing unto the Lord all the Earth*. Solomon is the third figure depicted.

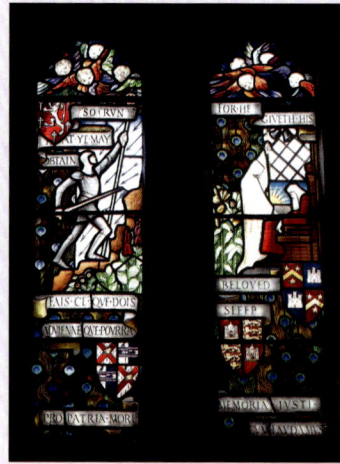

- **Hobson-O'Brien Window** (south-east chapel)
Two sisters, Emma Hobson and Mary O'Brien, are remembered here. The Biblical subjects are Elijah and a barrel of meal (Old Testament) and the Raising of Lazarus (New Testament). Overhead are the four evangelists, Matthew, Mark, Luke and John, while the tracery shows the emblems of Faith, Hope and Charity.

- **Barrington Window** (south-east chapel)
This window is in memory of Charlotte Barrington, wife of Sir Matthew Barrington.

Windows

- **Building of the Temple** (sanctuary east)
  In 480 BC, King Solomon began to build the Temple of the House of the Lord. It took seven years to complete (1 Kings 7).

- **O'Brien Memorial Window**
  (Harry Clarke Studio) (sanctuary)
  This three-light window commemorates Augustus Stafford O'Brien. He was noted for visiting the Crimea during the war there during the 19th century, administering help and comfort to the wounded and dying soldiers.
     The Biblical subjects represented include Our Lord seated overhead the charity of Dorcas and the Good Samaritan. Mr O'Brien took a practical interest in the Cathedral, including renovations.

Windows

ACKNOWLEDGEMENTS AND PHOTOGRAPHIC CREDITS

The Dean expresses his thanks to all those who contributed towards the production of this booklet: Rosalind Stevenson (Editor, The People, The Windows), Bishop Michael Burrows (Foreword and Misericords), John Elliott (A Brief History of an Ancient Cathedral), Andrea Brislane (A Brief History of an Ancient Cathedral), Jim Noonan (The Treasury), Noreen Ellerker (Monuments), Kieron Brislane (Bells), Peter Barley (Music), Craig Copley Brown (The Graveyard). Thanks also to John Holmes for his photography, and to the team in Kulturalis for their guidance and help.

All photographs by John Holmes, except for p.13 (bottom), Courtesy the National Library of Ireland; p.32 (bottom), Smith Archive / Alamy; images on pages 14 and 15 © Reproduced with the permission of the Representative Church Body of the Church of Ireland; and images on p.16 © Diocese of Limerick. O'Dea mitre and crosier are displayed in the Hunt Museum, Limerick on behalf of the diocese.

This edition © Kulturalis Ltd, 2026

Texts © the Dean and Chapter of Saint Mary's Cathedral, Limerick, 2026.
Illustrations © the Dean and Chapter of Saint Mary's Cathedral, Limerick, 2026, unless otherwise stated.

The author has asserted their rights under the Copyright, Designs and Patents Act, 1988, to be identified as the author of this work.

First published in 2026 by
Kulturalis Ltd
14 Old Queen Street
London SW1H 9HP
United Kingdom
www.kulturalis.com

ISBN 978-1-83636-015-5

Project manager: Neil Burkey
Designer: Adrian Hunt

Printed and bound in Turkey
Reproduction by Opero, Verona

10 9 8 7 6 5 4 3 2 1

EU GPSR Authorised Representative:
EASY ACCESS SYSTEM EUROPE OÜ,
Mustamäe tee 50, 10621, TALLINN, Estonia
email: info@easproject.org

All rights reserved. No part of this book may be reproduced, stored in a retrieval system or transmitted in any form or by any means electronic, mechanical, photocopying, recording or otherwise, without the written permission of the author and publisher.

Every effort has been made to acknowledge correct copyright of images where applicable. Any errors or omissions are unintentional and should be notified to the publisher, who will arrange for corrections to appear in any future editions.

British Library Cataloguing in Publication Data. A catalogue record for this book is available from the British Library.

50 FINDS FROM ESSEX
Objects from the Portable Antiquities Scheme

Ben Paites

AMBERLEY

First published 2016

Amberley Publishing
The Hill, Stroud
Gloucestershire, GL5 4EP

www.amberley-books.com

Copyright © Ben Paites, 2016

The right of Ben Paites to be identified as the
Author of this work has been asserted in accordance
with the Copyrights, Designs and Patents Act 1988.

ISBN 978 1 4456 5835 3 (print)
ISBN 978 1 4456 5836 0 (ebook)

All rights reserved. No part of this book may be
reprinted or reproduced or utilised in any form
or by any electronic, mechanical or other means,
now known or hereafter invented, including
photocopying and recording, or in any information
storage or retrieval system, without the permission
in writing from the Publishers.

British Library Cataloguing in Publication Data.
A catalogue record for this book is available from
the British Library.

Typeset in 10pt on 13pt Celeste.
Typesetting by Amberley Publishing.
Printed in the UK.

Appointed GPSR EU Representative: Easy Access
System Europe Oü, 16879218
Address: Mustamäe tee 50, 10621, Tallinn, Estonia
Contact Details: gpsr.requests@easproject.com,
+358 40 500 3575